KALEIDOSCOPE

CAERPHILLY

Edited by Dave Thomas

First published in Great Britain in 1999 by
POETRY NOW YOUNG WRITERS
Remus House, Coltsfoot Drive,
Woodston,
Peterborough, PE2 9JX
Telephone (01733) 890066

HB ISBN 0 75430 433 7
SB ISBN 0 75430 434 5

FOREWORD

This year, the Poetry Now Young Writers' Kaleidoscope competition proudly presents the best poetic contributions from over 32,000 up-and coming writers nationwide.

Successful in continuing our aim of promoting writing and creativity in children, each regional anthology displays the inventive and original writing talents of 11-18 year old poets. Imaginative, thoughtful, often humorous, *Kaleidoscope Caerphilly* provides a captivating insight into the issues and opinions important to today's young generation.

The task of editing inevitably proved challenging, but was nevertheless enjoyable thanks to the quality of entries received. The thought, effort and hard work put into each poem impressed and inspired us all. We hope you are as pleased as we are with the final result and that you continue to enjoy *Kaleidoscope Caerphilly* for years to come.

CONTENTS

Dean Huntley	70
Stacey Adams	71
Kwokwen Cheung	72
Nicola Banner-Martin	73
Gemma Ellis	74
David Rees	75
Tayona Powell	76
Daffydd Fones	77
Christine Partridge	78
Emma Kidley	79
Anna Matthews	80
Alexandra Lazarou	81
Samantha Weaver	82
Danielle L Braddon	83
Laura Morgan	84
Briony Laura Watkins	85
Jaclyn Skinner	86
Kyle Flew	87
Kirsty Graham	88
Simon Turner	89
Lesley Skipper	90
Jennifer Lock	91
Adam Young	92
Donna Stuart	93
Sarah Alderman	94
Sarah Lenderyou	95
Christopher Jones	96
Kirstin Hampton	97
Cheryl Jackson	98
Cara Dee Starr	99
Liz Gregor	100
Gavin Williams	101
Danielle Perrett	102
Emily King	103
Keelan Bailey	104
Steven Morgan	105

The Poems

THE BRIBE

After exams -
> you can do as you please
> you can do it all then
> you can visit your friends
> you can stay out till ten.

After exams -
> you can do as you like
> you can play table tennis
> dismantle your bike

> Spend the day at the swimming pool
> hang round the shops
> you can fool with the dog
> and watch Top of the Pops.

After exams -
> we may even allow
> the party you mentioned -
> but please revise *now*.

Tammy McCarthy (12)

ANGELIC SUNSET

As the tide comes in
the sand patterns are washed away
White streaks of foam
edge the rippling waves
in the angelic sunset.

Poised in the pink night sky
sits the elegant master of the universe
sending out a shimmering glow
which lights up the golden beach
in the angelic sunset.

The sea is now calm and still
the sky turns into a blanket
of navy blue and silver dots
which is the concluding part
of an angelic sunset.

Laura Jenkins (12)

THE GRINNING MOON

The field is like a pool of silver,
the moon like a disc in the sky.

Then a happy little star steps
into the spotlight,
and gives a little cheer then a grin.

The moon does its act,
then broadens his face,
as if the man on the moon was really there.

Emma Bridges (13)

FUN!

Fun can be anything, anything at all.
Fun can be a hobby, netball, hockey and football.
You could play board games to pass time.
Fun can last forever, and forever it will remain.
After school and we have done our homework
my mum always says 'Go on go and have some
                    Fun!'

Joanna Jenkins (12)

AUTUMN

I woke up this morning full of glee,
until I realised it wasn't sunny.
When I looked out my window I couldn't see
the birds singing merrily.
They were all hiding in their nests
I was beginning to miss what I'd before called pests.
Whatever happened to the sun that shone
in the deep blue sky?
All I could see was frost and grey mist through my eye.
The trees have lost their leaves and the flowers are dead,
There was no sign of any creatures in the flower bed.
Autumn has come and winter is here,
it's going to be wind and rain through to next year.
Until the spring comes back
I suggest we all invest in an umbrella and a waterproof mac.

Kirsty Herrin (12)

TITANIC IS DEAD

The dark eerie ghost-ship lies undisturbed on the sea bed.
A lifeless, rotting wreck where happiness once bubbled.
Belongings from the rich and poor, old and young,
lay broken on the sea bed where they fell years ago.

In the distance the piercing shrieks can still be heard and the
unanswered calls for people - some lost forever.
The splashes, the panic, the fear, then the sorrow,
all come to the brave and the cowardly alike.

Now the dark waters gently flow over her,
letting her rest peacefully and calmly.
Nothing passes, nothing stirs
over her watery grave.

Hannah Feldon (12)

SCHOOL

We wake up early every day
To catch the bus to school.
We go to registration
Every day to see if we are here.
So here come the lessons,
The first two,
Welsh and English.
Then it's time for break,
Then it's French and science,
Lunch is next.
Tuck-shop opens every day
With food for you to eat.
Then it's RE,
Off home with lots of homework,
And same again tomorrow!

Eleri Jenkins (12)

TRAVELLING

In my car I'm travelling away,
Away I flee.
I can't sleep for interest is tickling my brain.
The trees aren't brown stumps and green leaves.
As far as I can see red and burnt orange leaves scatter.
Brown and a colour on its own take over the bark.

People I see playing happily,
Going to town and talking to each other.
Fighting going on in the back, I can't stay here much longer.
I slip from reality and fall asleep.
My mind just thinks, it collects my thoughts together,
It makes those colours, pictures and landscapes come back.

I get to my destination at last.
How I wonder, what my next journey will bring.
Will I see trees, people and colours?
Would I just not take notice?
Was that journey made for me or was I imagining?
I wait for what my next journey brings.
Will that one be for me?

Ceinwen Howell (11)

CELEBRATIONS

Everybody likes a celebration,
They are very exciting times.
Weddings, christenings and birthdays,
Brings everyone a smile.

Party-poppers never stop,
Get out all the wine.
Celebrations in the air
Toasts and speeches all the time.

At the end of the party
Pick up all the mess.
Everyone has a good time,
Well more or less.

Rachel Davies (11)

POLLUTION

An unsightly clutter,
of foul trash,
murdering nature and
destroying our almost perfect environment.

Contaminating the air,
with fatal chemicals,
uncertain,
of the consequences that could occur.

Rejecting refuse,
into the sea,
slaughtering sea life,
selfishly.

In the future who knows,
a world of shamble,
an inconsiderate, reckless community,
thoughtless of what they affect.

Nicola Preece (12)

A HEDGEHOG

A simple ball of prickly spines,
With four legs and a nose,
At night he'll rummage for his food,
In daylight he will doze.

Wiggly worms and slippery snails,
And he will have a feast,
A million spikes he seems to have
Or a hundred at the least.

He creeps around silently,
Without a single sound,
He hides in bushes and bracken,
So he won't be found.

In the cold he will sleep,
Outside he won't go.
Not in the rain, wind or sleet,
Especially not in snow.

Helen Irving (12)

Fox

As its eyes glittered in the night
giving you quite a fright
As the shining white moon looked down upon
that cuddly looking fox was gone.

Creeping slowly through the wood
catching something looking good
Not stirring a single leaf
acting like a cunning thief.

Gliding, swiftly across the fields
steadily at its victim's heels
But oh suddenly we hear the horseshoes thud
the horns blowing while splattering through the mud.

The people in red coats chasing through the fields
and woods and mountains with no protection or shield.
Its flaming red coat glimmering in the sun
now it's dangerous, he's on the run.

The pack of those bloodthirsty hounds
catching up, bringing that fox to the ground
But that cunning fox he slipped away
and forever climbed the mountains, I'm glad to say.

Jennifer Organ (12)

THE BUTTERFLY

My favourite is the butterfly,
All colours on its wings,
I love to see it fly,
Up high into the sky.

Its colours are so bright,
But it's not seen in the night.
We only see it in the day,
When we are out at play.

How pretty the butterfly is,
When its wings are a whizz,
It's so happy flying along,
Like someone singing a song.

The legs are so tiny,
The wings are so shiny,
The body has spots,
Amongst all the dots.

Carrie-Ann Davies (12)

WALES

Wales is the place for hills and valleys,
Daffodils and leeks,
Wales is where you'll find wet weather,
It rains for weeks and weeks.

Wales is where you'll find great traditions,
For folk songs and folk dancing,
With an Eisteddfod every year,
There'll be something you'll want to win.

Wales is the place to wear a red shirt,
And start a game of rugby,
With the Cardiff Devils and Michael Owen,
We like other sports too, you'll see.

Wales is where you'll find great music,
Tom Jones, Shirley Bassey too,
Catatonia and the Manic Street Preachers,
Stereophonics we love you.

With its unpronounceable names
And brilliant language too,
Wales is a fantastic country,
I'm proud to be Welsh. Are you?

Hayley Bennett (12)

ON CHRISTMAS NIGHT

Girls and boys rush up to bed
With only Santa in their head,
Shut their eyes and fall asleep
As they know St Nick will creep.

Sleigh bells ringing in the snow
Though the children should not know.
Dasher, Dancer, Prancer, Vixen
Comet, Cupid, Donna, Blitzen.

Landing on the rooftops
Giving presents to all the tots,
Placing them under the tree,
Children's faces filled with glee.

Santa's job has been fun
A year to go until another one.

Sarah Cowley (13)

THE BALLET CLASS

My teacher's name is Mr Fasor,
(You say it so it rhymes with razor).
When I was five he used to say,
'You'll be in the Royal Ballet one day!'
But I'm still here, I'm now thirteen,
But I don't mind I'm still quite keen.

My good friend Holly she went far,
She'll soon become a dancing star.
She went away to ballet school,
And now she's there she thinks it's cool.

I'll never be quite good enough,
To mess around with all that stuff,
I'll keep on twice a week,
And hope one day I'll reach my peak.

Old Fasor tries his very best,
But my class put him to the test,
When we do our plies and jumps,
He says we're like great big lumps.

We go up on point and do our rises,
Causing one or two surprises!
Our legs turned in and they're like jelly,
Our bottoms are out and so is my belly.

When the lesson is at an end,
We're supposed to stretch and bend,
But Fasor's always far too late
To stop us getting through the gate.
Although we're tired and complain,
We'll always go back there again.

Alys Hempstead (13)

THE ICEBERG

The black waves rise and fall around
the beautiful ice maiden.
An object can be seen through
the clear night sky.
The stars flicker and the moon
illuminates the emptiness of the ocean.
The shadow slowly approaches
the gleaming jagged iceberg.
She reaches across its metal side,
breaking the silence of the crisp cold night.
She watches as the ship slips to its grave.
Drawing her arm back to her side,
she feels her amazing power,
and sits tall in her glory.
She belonged to the ocean,
but the ocean was hers.

Charlotte Gooding (13)

LIFE

Life is hard
Don't you agree
Life is hard
It makes us think
Life is hard
It gives us things to handle.

Life is fun
Don't you agree
Life is fun
It's just like a mystery
Life is fun
We can enjoy it to the full

Life is full of challenges
Don't you agree
Life is full of challenges
All to be enjoyed
Life is full of challenges
Just you wait and see.

Kirsty Halliday (12)

POETRY

Poems are really hard to write,
Still I try and try with all of my might,
I think and think for hours on end,
It nearly drives me round the bend.

I sit in my bedroom day after day,
Trying to think of what to say,
I look at it when it's finally done,
And I see that I need a much better one.

I work deep into the night,
Trying to get it perfectly right,
And after all of my hard work,
I end up looking like a jerk,
Because when I hand my poem in,
It ends up going right in the bin!

Kirsty Robinson (12)

OBSERVATIONS AT A POETRY WORKSHOP

At length the 'poet' praised the sun's beams
Which bandaged her in a deep abyss
Of her own self-satisfaction.
Her saccharin superficial statement
'The world is a beautiful place,'
Jarred the essence of the Japanese director and poet
Like the delicate patter of the crimson leaves
Which scuttle against Herculean walls.
His voice disputed 'I am not so hasty . . .'

The figure of a woman, her widespread arms
Silhouetted against the kaleidoscopic madness
Of the swarming streets.
A lemon plunges from her hand
Like a bomb.
As her face crumples
Like discarded rubbish in the gutter
And her world erupts around her . . .

'No' repeated the poet. 'I am not so hasty.'

Zoe Brigley (17)

FIREWORKS

F ireworks are so much fun
I n the night it looks like the sun
R eally is a lot of fun
E verybody comes to see them
W e love fireworks
O ver the world they will fly
R ound and round they will go
K issing when no one knows
S uddenly they explode.

Bethan Evans (12)

MY MUM

I love my mum because she's sweet.
She isn't sour, she's just sweet,
a beautiful lady and my best friend.
I will always love her to the bitter end
because she will always be my best friend.

Emily Clement (12)

HALLOWE'EN

Hallowe'en is a fun night
All the children and adults
In their wonderful costumes
I like masks and funny noses
Only children do trick or treat
When people are at home
Everyone listens for the knock
Even grown-ups join in the fun
No one is left out.

Matthew Lewis (13)

PUMPKINS

P umpkins everywhere, children lighting them,
U sually bought for Hallowe'en.
M ums and dads gouge them out,
P eople and pumpkins everywhere.
K ids running round, knocking door to door.
I nside the house the pumpkin is a dimming light,
N ights getting darker and darker,
S oon it will be winter.

Daniel Green (12)

STAYING DOWN

I love sleeping down my Aunty Tina's for the weekend,
She's the coolest adult I know.
Do you want to say down too?
Ok, better hurry though,
I'm about to go.

First I'll help my Uncle Tim put up his mini carousel,
Then I'll play Frisbee with my cousins and their neighbours.
Come on let's have a game of tag,
Or chase Woody round the football field.

It's dark now, let's go in, play on the Sega
Or listen to CDs.
Come on it's one o'clock in the morning,
And Tina spotted a fox!
You've got to be quiet if you want to see it,
It's got cubs with it.

I could watch the foxes all night with Tina,
Or challenge her to pool,
She always wins though,
Even if we play by my rules!

Joanne Taylor (12)

ELEPHANTS

The elephants' tusks are like hardened snow,
The giant of Africa roams his land.
His ears like flags, flapping in the wind,
His trunk twisting and turning like a snake,
Slithering from side to side.
He's looking for peace,
Peace to be able to live from the perils of man.

Alun Jones (13)

MY TIGER

He reminds me of an orange zebra crossing.
Standing proud on the ground,
Prowls in long thick green grass.
Chases after his prey,
It never gets away.
He looks like a fire burning through the night,
If you walk into him,
He'll give you such a fright.

Siân Green (12)

CATS

Cats sleep anywhere,
Any shoe,
Any chair,
Top of table,
Behind a cupboard.

Cats hunt anywhere,
Any garden,
Any place,
They hunt for mice,
Behind the stairs,
Their claws as sharp as razors.

Sara Petherick (11)

HALLOWE'EN

Vampire bats flying through the sky
Witches on their brooms
The Devil sitting down below
Ghosts flying, dark at night
Dracula flying round and round
Vampires lying in their coffins tonight.

Samantha Hawthorne (11)

WHALES

The sea is like a supermarket,
With every variety of whale.
Killer whales, as black as coal,
Their stomach is as white as snow,
Big blue whales
As blue as the summer sky,
Humpback whales, so sweet, big
And as bold as brass.
I think whales are beautiful
So big and cute
I love whales.

Natasha Newbury (13)

CHEETAH

I love the way they run
smoothly through the grass,
They chase after their prey
which probably tastes scrumptious,
Their brightly coloured coats
yellow with black spots,
They run so fast,
The prey can't get away,
They can run as fast as a train.
What are they?
Cheetahs.

Kerry Price (13)

RYAN GIGGS

He's as fast as a leopard,
Skills like magic,
Football.
Pride of Manchester and Wales,
Red.
17 years old made his debut,
Amazing?
I'd love to meet him,
Ryan Giggs, Manchester United.

David Sparey (11)

HALLOWE'EN

People dress up like witches and vampires,
even Dracula
with blood down their face.
Sticks with a skull on the top,
Devils which have come from hell
just to trick or treat.
Some stay in for candy and ducking apples,
and some think that it is fun to throw eggs
at other people but not me.
And just to finish this scary night when the clock
reaches midnight you'll be in for a fright
because you will hear a werewolf howl.
You will not sleep a wink.

Scott Williams (11)

THE WRITER OF THIS POEM

The writer of this poem,
Is fatter than a pig,
As beautiful as a princess,
As sharp as a nib.

As friendly as a mouse,
As wet as a fish,
As warm as a house,
As hard as a dish.

As happy as a birthday,
As wise as an owl,
As good as gold,
As soft as a towel.

The writer of this poem
Is faster than a cheetah,
As brave as a lion,
As smart as a teacher.

Laura Nicholas (12)

HALLOWE'EN

The skies are as dark as coal.
The streets are roaming with werewolves.
Vampires have blood dripping from their mouths.
Red Devils are trick or treating.
There are witches flying on their brooms.
The houses are haunted and spooky.
Kids egging houses.
Oooow!

Jamie Green (11)

MUM

My mum is beautiful
As beautiful as a rose in spring
She is as funny as can be
She is as loving as a kitten
Every time I see my mother
I am happy as a swan.

Natasha Deane (11)

HALLOWE'EN

People knock on my door and they looked spooky.
A boy looked like a devil.
A girl had a scary mask on.
It looked haunted.
Someone had blood down his face.
It looked as if the monster was real.
A vampire came to my door.
A bunch of witches were walking around.
A boy looked like Einstein.
A black cat was as black as night.
A bunch of witches were going trick or treat.
A hairy wolf was on top of the mountain.

Michael Mordecai (11)

RED

Red is like sunset
So beautiful and bright
It's as happy as Santa on Christmas Eve night
It's as hot as a fire, giving out light
Red is the colour of love and romance.

Julie Jenkins (11)

SNAKES

Like big slow worms,
Twisting around each tree,
Killing their prey,
With their knifelike teeth.
Fangs poisonous and fatal,
Different colours: the patterns on them look like a map,
Yellow, red, green and black,
Like big tree veins
Bulging out of each tree.

Their tongues big and red, used to sample air.
Their eyes are like marbles,
Giving you an evil stare.

Helen Davis (12)

WHEELS

The wheels spin around, like a washing machine.
The blade on the lawnmower spins around to cut the grass.
Skates go rolling down the hill tumbling over the stones
They spin around like lightning.
Psychedelic shades on the wheel trim
Blend into one amazing colour.

Christopher Morgan (11)

HALLOWE'EN

The evil Devil
The witch's black cats
The bats are black
The spooky ghosts
Some slimy monster
And some evil spells
Lots of blood
Dracula's teeth are as sharp as a knife.

Scott Morgan (11)

WITCHES

W itches are so cruel
I gnore them flying through the air
T esting their powers on little children
C atching anyone they can to eat
H orrible to think about
E arly eerie sounds at night
S tomachs frying in a pan.

Scott Thomas (11)

HALLOWE'EN

H ave fun on the special day
A ll children like to dress up!
L aughing, giggling and eating candy
L urking around corners to jump out on people
O h no, it's that time of year again
W itches with broomsticks, knocking doors
E gging people's houses, running away
E very adult stays indoors
N aughty, spooky children knocking and running away.

Carl Atwood (11)

SWEETS

Sweets are scrumptious to eat.
Some are long and thin,
Others are quite round,
Some go *bang!* Some go *pop!*
Others don't make a sound!
Some tickle as they go down your throat.

Keighley Greening (11)

BOOKS

Enchanting tales of magic,
Legends of new and old,
Stories happy and stories tragic,
Comics - big, brave and bold.

Novels of heart-warming fiction,
Mysteries of unresolved crime,
Excitement, love and addiction,
Get stuck in a book for all time!

Michelle Ward (14)

THE ALIEN

As I fly through the galaxy
I see many animals great and small
But look at me I'm very tall

I fly to the moon
I fly quite fast
And leave places I've been in the past

My rocket is red
With black and green dots
But I am purple with Technicolor spots

I am an alien to you
And you are to me
But what you get is what you see

I have to go now
I won't be back soon
I will send you a postcard when I get to the moon.

Matthew Ridout (13)

A Cat's Life

Being a cat is such a good life,
I have no worry, have no strife.
My coat is glossy,
My eyes are bright,
I really am a wonderful sight.
My food and milk appear each day,
I do no work, I earn no pay.
I sleep all day in my favourite chair,
Disturb me - no, they wouldn't dare.

When I awake I groom my coat,
For other cats to come and gloat.
When night-time comes I try to hide,
For that's the time I'm put outside.
I hear the footsteps on the floor,
Next thing I know I'm *out the door.*

Claire Perry (12)

KITTY

Probably the laziest cat here in Hillside Park,
Doesn't really go outside,
But doesn't mind a fight,
No other cat can come on her land,
No other cat can threaten her,
No other cat is so frightened of my dad,
When my dad walks through the door.

My cat really loves my mother,
My mother really loves my cat,
The only thing about this cat is that she always
Brings in slowworms.
My dad chucks them outside as well as my cat,
My cat doesn't like this
And always comes back.

Lisa Davis (12)

FEAR

Fear is the colour black.
It is a big fat bat.
It is being lost in a maze
without anyone to help.
Fear is a hairy face
with no features.
It is the smell of burning flesh.
It is seeing your life being a mess.

Richard Toghill (12)

The Greatest Game

Football is the greatest game
All the others compared are lame
Feel the ball at your feet
It's like the feeling of sucking a real good sweet
Sprinting down the wing
The crowd starts to scream and sing
Williams crosses the ball into the box
By centimetres it skims my socks
The goalkeeper runs out
Punches me in the face
Knocks me out
Cole goes for the goal
But he misses and it hits the pole
The ball comes back out
The crowd starts to shout
Williams takes a swing
The ball goes in
Hooray we win!

Leigh Williams (12)

MY LIFE

I like computers very much,
Hours on end of joy,
Three Lions is my best,
Scoring all the time.

My mum and dad are crazy,
So is my brother too,
They're always having curries,
And running to the loo.

My brother is always nasty,
Pinching all my things,
He's beating me up all the time,
And is a bad sportsman.

Anthony Henderson (12)

MY MAGIC WAND

Oh magic wand
Make me pretty
Mix me up a magic powder
Use some stars and use some moon
You can even throw in a magic broom
Cut them up into little pieces and stir them around
Until stirred a hundred times
Add some water add some milk
Put it in a bottle for me to drink
Say the magic word so I will sleep
Put me in an enchanted wood
Wake me up in a thousand years
Then I shall be the prettiest in the world.

Lisa Verity (11)

HALLOWE'EN

Hallowe'en is coming,
Get ready for it,
Make your costumes, there are plenty to choose from,
Witches, Devils and all sorts.
When you go out be very careful,
Knock people's doors and say 'Trick or treat.'
You may get candy or money,
Then go home and eat them all,
Spend your money the next day!

Emma Davies (13)

WINTER WONDERLAND

White sheet of silk on all the shops,
Ice-cold weather,
Naughty children throwing snowballs,
Things turn white in the winter,
Everything all quiet,
Rivers turn into ice rinks.

Laura Hopkins (13)

HALLOWE'EN

H appy children knocking on doors

A ll shouting 'Trick or treat'

L oony outfits, funny make-up

L eaping from door to door to get their candy

O ut of all the nights this has to be the best

W itches with green hair

E ggs flying around everywhere

E very child's dream is here tonight because they love candy

N aughty pranks and tricks are played on Hallowe'en night.

Rachel Evans (13)

HALLOWE'EN

H allowe'en is a brilliant time
A ngry children throwing eggs
L ittle children in costumes
L ying, rolling on the ground
O ver houses away they go
W hisking away on broomsticks
E gged windows in a mess
E veryone cleaning up
N ever go out on . . . Hallowe'en.

Simon Hinton (13)

HALLOWE'EN

Hallowe'en children all dressed up
trick or treating collecting sweets in a cup.
Hallowe'en, as dark as a black cat
hunting for prey.
Hallowe'en, ghosts raising from the dead -
So you'd better stay in bed!

Charlotte Lamch (14)

FEAR

Fear is frightening,
Dark and bitter,
It makes monsters appear,
Monsters with big yellow teeth,
Red eyes and blood dripping everywhere!
People are afraid of fear.

Jason Cooper (14)

WHAT'S REALLY PUT INTO A FAIRY TALE

Gallant knights dashing through forests to save princesses,
Scorching dragons stopping them in their tracks,
Princesses as beautiful as red roses,
Ugly witches, ugly enough to smash glass,
Handsome princes, the sort princesses sigh for,
Enchanted forests that are open to everyone,
Nasty gremlins which are short and stumpy,
Flying unicorns as white as snow,
Golden palaces where the romance takes
                               place in all fairy tales.

Nassir Domun (11)

RECIPE FOR A FAIRY TALE

Recipe: Take a prince and a princess,
              Then put in a talking dragon,
              Then throw in a spotty witch
              Who tries to kill the princess.
              Then put in a fairy godmother,
              And a rainbow potion.

Method: Leave under the moonlight for 100 years.

Result: A prince saving the princess, getting married
              And living happily ever after.

Dane Gibbs (11)

BONFIRE NIGHT

The night is a fright like a fight
With all fireworks in the sky,
When all the kids are loving it to bits,
While the grown-ups do not like it,
All the people in their houses
Trying to have peace and quiet,
While they hear *bang, bang, bang!*

Geraint Williams

OCTOBER 31ST

October 31st has come around again,
Witches fly through the night,
Little children full of fright,
Black cats
With bright green eyes,
They're watching every move you make,
Sort of like a slithering snake,
Bats hiding in dark holes of trees,
Vampires waiting on a perch,
For humans they shall search,
Hallowe'en, Hallowe'en
Has come around again.

Penny Holborn (11)

FEAR

Eyes to frighten
Turn and twist
Grip to tighten
A blinding mist

> Sharp as a knife
> Like a bad dream
> As real as life
> Run and scream

A distant howl
In the night
The fears prowl
Gives a fright

> There's a bump!
> The morning is near
> Followed by a thump
> The sound of fear

Crawl and stagger
Here comes fear
A pointed dagger
Fear is here!

Kirsty Ellis (11)

FRIENDS

Friends are always there for you,
Sharing gifts and secrets too,
They never lie or pinch your sweets,
They are always there when you need help,
Telling jokes when school is out,
On the bus they sit by you,
Giving chewing gum, and the flu,
They comfort you when you're scared
And always make you be prepared,
They notice when you are down
And wrap you in a dressing gown.

Sarah Hughes (12)

Cats

Eyes as big as saucepans,
Tongues as sharp as spikes
Prowling through the moonlight
At midnight
Pouncing on mice
Birds and dogs too
Sometimes they might even chase you!

Sophie Hodges (11)

MY FRIEND JENNY

My friend Jenny is always there,
my friend Jenny always seems to care.
Even when we scream and shout,
we always seem to work things out.

She has brown frizzy hair,
she'd look rather strange if it wasn't there.
She lends me money,
if she has any spare,
but usually her pockets are bare.

Without Jenny as my friend,
my life would surely come to an end.
Thank you Jenny for all you've done,
my life with you is so much fun.

Now my poem has come to an end,
so thank you Jenny for being my friend.

Kelly Woolley (13)

FIRE

Fire is hot and burns your soul,
Fire will swallow you like a hole,
Fire will burn you like the sun,
Fire is deadly and kills all life,
Fire will destroy everything in its path,
Fire is like a blaze of light,
Fire keeps you warm in the wintry sun,
Firefighters keep the fire under control.

Thomas Llewellyn (12)

BROTHERS

Brothers - who needs them?
Me, that's who.
I know I say I hate them, but I don't think I do,
Even though Gareth hits me,
And wherever I go, Ryan follows too.
I know I love my brothers
And I think they like me too.

Laura Claire Davies (12)

HALLOWE'EN

My third favourite night of the year,
Children all dressed up as witches, wolves and ghosts,
'Trick or treat,' they always say,
With Jack-o-lanterns by their faces,
Lots of sweets in their pockets.

In the house they always play ducking
and hanging apples,
It's always fun to play and it's always
    Spooky!

Daniel Butler (11)

HALLOWE'EN

H allowe'en is a laugh.
A dults hardly like it.
L oads of people run around.
L ots of money given away.
O n this night you get a fright.
W e have fun.
'E ar the children screaming, shouting.
'E ar and see loads of children.
N ow we shall go to bed!

Dean Huntley (11)

HALLOWE'EN

H allowe'en, Hallowe'en,
A ll the witches laugh and scream,
L ittle children all around,
L onely houses spooky and cold,
O n the streets the witches call,
W earing hats and cloaks all black,
E ating apples with a cat,
E ven though they try to trick you,
N ever let a witch put a spell on you.

Stacey Adams (14)

FORESTRY

It is full of surprises,
Animals roaming around freely,
A habitat for most,
Growing food like mushrooms,
Rotting wood on the ground,
The smell of damp leaves
that gives you a bit of a buzz!

The night gives you a fright,
Owls watching over you,
Wolves howling in the moonlit sky,
Cats running from place to place,
Animals and creatures come out for food!

In the light it is bright,
Too bright to look up,
You'll wonder when you'll find something nice,
Even a place for a den,
A quiet place to relax,
A place for fun and laughter,
Most of all it makes a better world!

Kwokwen Cheung (12)

THE BULLY

What is a bully?
Is it someone who is just mean?
Or is it someone who is lonely?
Someone without any friends,
Only does it to be popular.

It might be someone who is just cruel,
Every time they see someone they
just have to hit them,
Someone who can't control their temper.

Is it someone who is jealous?
Jealous of people who have more than themselves,
They don't like others because they have
more than they do,
What is a bully?
It's not me or you!

Nicola Banner-Martin (12)

POEM

I was told to write a poem,
So that is what I'll do.
I don't know what to write about,
I haven't got a clue!

I'll think hard all of the night,
And then even the day.
I was told to write a poem,
In a poem kind of way.

I could write about a fight,
Football, a group or ghost.
I'd better decide quickly,
Which idea I like the most.

My poem is coming to an end,
To write a poem 'how'?
I guess I'll never find out,
So I'd better finish now.

Gemma Ellis (13)

BEANO

B army characters
E xtremely daft stories
A nd read by everyone including people who drive lorries
N o boring stuff and
O ut of bounds to dull people.

David Rees (12)

A SIGN OF THE TIMES

Murder, arson, burglary, this country's in a plight
Drugs, drink, child abuse, and teenagers with the need to fight
Elderly people living in fear, is it any wonder why
When crime against the elderly has never been so high

It doesn't help when policemen are being taken off the street
All because the government can't make their figures meet
We're all in a vicious circle, unemployment, no hope, prison
Put away your indignation, it's time to stop and listen
How can we solve it? What's the answer? A miracle maybe
I'm afraid that's probably something none of us will ever see

'Bring back the birch and hanging,' the older generation cry
Yes the young are unruly, but stop and reason why
When you were young you didn't wonder who dad was, you know
Necessity kept families together, divorces were very few

Times were hard, money short, but it didn't seem to matter
You had security with a mum and dad who listened to your chatter
There was no television or money to smoke and drink
You weren't left for hours, no one caring if you'd swim or sink
Or living on a council estate with a single parent on the brink

So next time you're called names, by hooligans passing by
It shouldn't make you angry, it should make you want to cry.

Tayona Powell (12)

HALLOWE'EN

Every Hallowe'en I dress up as a 'dead' being.
Everybody screams the houses down.
When we go home we eat our treats.
We gave some tricks and laughed to bits.
Now it's time to go to sleep.

Daffydd Fones (13)

LOVE

I really love this boy at school,
He makes my colours all stand out.
He lives on a different estate
But I don't care.
I can always look forward to tomorrow.

Sometimes I wonder, does he love me?
But then I see him with another girl.
I don't know love.
But they do - I wish I was her.

Christine Partridge (13)

FRIENDS

Some friends are enemies
Wicked and unkind
Some friends are happy
Thoughts stirring in your mind
All mixed together
The best friends they
Would be
We all laugh together
In a musical harmony
We had happy and
Sad times, warm
And some cold
But if I lost my friend
I'd lose my heart of gold.

Emma Kidley (13)

WINTER

Winter is a ghost,
rushing through every corner.
Winter is a fluffy white carpet,
covering the flowers until warm spring comes.
Winter is ice left in a freezer,
when spring comes, it appears in her warm green coat.
'Plants,' she will say, 'it's time to grow.'

Anna Matthews (13)

THE GREEN LADY'S LAMENT

Over the battlements she strolls,
Dressed in long green flowing robes,
She walks the tower every night,
Awaiting her beloved knight.

The castle brings pain and strife,
To one accustomed to a colourful life,
Her efforts to make it a joyful place,
Guilbert de Claire thought a disgrace.

Soon a Welsh prince came to these parts,
And fell in love with Alice de la Marche,
She returned his love and soon they found,
They were meeting each other underground.

Guilbert found out about their affair,
And sent her to France he did not care,
There she died of a broken heart,
Banished from her love. Forever apart.

Alexandra Lazarou (12)

DREAMLAND

Where shall I go when I dream today?
Under the sea so far away,
Where the dolphins brush past,
And the crabs scurry fast,
That's where I'll go today.

Maybe I'll journey to outer space,
I won't be the first in the human race,
I'll visit Jupiter, Pluto and Mars,
Then travel to other distant stars,
That's where I'll go today.

Into the country I'll wander and roam,
Where I'll watch a blue bird building its home,
Flowers I'll see, then butterflies and bees
Cascading around the old oak trees,
That's where I'll go today.

Oh how I love to dream,
About where I'm going or where I've been,
But I think I'd rather go to bed,
Have a soft pillow beneath my head,
That's where I'll go tonight.

Samantha Weaver (11)

HALLOWE'EN

H allowe'en is great fun
A nd scary sometimes too
L ovely sweets from trick or treating
L ove to scare on Hallowe'en
O nly when it's midnight I go out
W hen a spine-chilling full moon appears
E erie noises can be heard
E ven when the night disappears
N othing ever scares me because I love
    Hallowe'en.

Danielle L Braddon (11)

MY NAN'S A SUPERHERO

My nan's a superhero,
She's the best a nan can be,
She really is terrific,
And she really loves me.

She wears her frilly knickers
Outside her dressing gown,
If you didn't know her,
You'd think she was a clown.

But I know my nan's the best,
And I think she's really great,
She'll always be my superhero,
My very greatest mate.

Laura Morgan (11)

BONFIRE NIGHT

Bonfire night is the fifth of November,
This is a date I'll always remember.
For this is the day on which I was born,
Bonfires! Hot dogs! It's never a yawn.
I watch the fireworks lighting up the sky,
Outside my window passing by.
When I'm lying in my bed,
So many colours; green, blue, and red.
But to celebrate my birthday I prefer a special meal,
Than going to see the rocket and Catherine wheel.
My own special reason to remember
The fifth of November.

Briony Laura Watkins (11)

FIREWORKS

F ireworks are lots of fun
I   n the sky I watch them glow
R oaring flames of the bonfire
E erie nights, cold and dark
W hirling Catherine wheels
O verhead colourful flames burn
R ound and round the fireworks spin
K eep away from the fireworks
S parkly spirals spinning in the sky.

Jaclyn Skinner (11)

FOUND

F inding things is very good.
O ver here and over there, finding things everywhere.
U nder here and under there, finding things everywhere.
N ever here, never there, losing things everywhere.
D on't do this, don't do that, find any money give it back.

Kyle Flew (11)

HALLOWE'EN

A noise, a scream,
A person unseen,
A scratch, an itch,
The laugh of a witch,
A scare, a fright,
On Hallowe'en night.

Kirsty Graham (11)

BATTLE SCARS

My mum said 'Look at you,
Your legs are black and blue,
You skin is raw,
They look so sore,
Whatever did you do?'

I turned to her and said
'Mum, we knocked them dead,
We scored three tries,
Before their eyes,
It's gone right to my head.'

Oh what a match it was,
You'd be so proud because
I ducked and ran,
And beat my man,
And scored another try.

Oh how they clapped and cried
The others on my side,
We're such good chums,
Even in the scrums,
If you see us run and hide!

We are the boys in green,
And we're the winning team,
Mr Lyons, he's just great,
We like to think that he's our mate,
He makes us really keen.

So never mind my cuts,
Although you'll think I'm nuts,
I live for rugby every day,
I'm only happy when I play
So no more ifs and buts.

Simon Turner (12)

My Spell Poem

Human's eye, squashed and roasted.
When the cauldron bubbles, it will be toasted.

A slimy human's bloody eye rolling across the floor.
Slimy fat white slugs creeping up a sliced back.

Human's eye, squashed and roasted.
When the cauldron bubbles, it will be toasted.

The remains of a baby's lips crawling along the door.
A large hairy spider's leg ripping out your heart.

Human's eye, squashed and roasted.
When the witches cackle, you know it's been toasted.

Lesley Skipper (12)

SPORT

S occer is like life, it's goals that count
P laying the game, to score the full amount
O bstacles are put in your way,
   once over them it's a great day
R ugby is played with an egg-shaped ball
   which is kicked between 'II' shaped post,
   ever so tall
T ennis with racket in hand, hit ball over net,
   it's forty-love - game, match and set.

Jennifer Lock (13)

FOREST HUNTER

I slither through the forest
Hunting for my prey
Up the tree and down the branch
Searching everywhere
I finally find my victim
Up high in a tree
Slowly, quietly I climb higher
Quickly I wrap myself around my victim
Squeezing tighter and tighter
My victim breathes its last breath
Then with one bite he's gone.

What am I?

Adam Young (12)

DREAM

There is a place
In a far away land
Where the beaches are of golden sand
All day long the sun shines bright
And the stars always shine at night
In this land nobody has troubles
Because all of the troubles fade like bubbles
Here everyone is friends
Their friendship never ends
Then sadly I wake and remember this place
But this brings sadness to my face
Because this place is so exciting
And our world is full of wars and fighting.

Donna Stuart (12)

MY HAMSTER

Fluffy, soft, playful, small,
as it curls himself
like a round ball.
As he is snuggled up in
his comfy bed
he sleeps peacefully
through the day.
 But in the night it turns
 into a loud
 rushing Gladiator
 as it runs on its wheel.
 I just wish I could
 get some sleep
 for once in my life!

Sarah Alderman (12)

Horse Let's Ride

H orses are beautiful animals,
O ne will do for me,
R ide through the autumn forest,
S ide by side we'll run together free,
E very day we will be together.

L et's ride through the night,
E verything we'll do together,
T wo of us side by side,
S ee your mane blowing smoothly in the wind.

R ide, ride, ride with me,
I n the blowing wind at night,
D rift into the windy night,
E ven if we've had so much fun.

Sarah Lenderyou (12)

I LIKE

I like just about everything
Anything at all
Like science, cheese and fish and even football
Take away the things I like
There would be nothing left at all.

Christopher Jones (13)

FRIENDS

Best friends are there when you need them,
Best friends are there when you don't,
Best friends are there when you wanna throw up,
And best friends are there when you don't.
So basically I'm saying to hold onto your friends,
Do not squabble or fight at every weekend,
And you will find that you can always depend on your
            Friends.

Kirstin Hampton (12)

BREAKFAST

Beep! Beep! The alarm clock goes.
I can hear something downstairs.
What is it? Nobody knows.

I make my way to the staircase top.
I can hear a sound, a crackle then a pop.

I hear the kettle whistling sharply.
I can almost taste the melted butter on toast.
The salty bacon I love the most.

I drift into the kitchen,
The sweet tastes and smells take me.
I love all of these especially my mum
For the breakfast she makes me.

Cheryl Jackson (12)

FRIENDSHIP

Friendship is a special thing
It gives happiness a little zing
Many people mean so much to me
Unhappy is not what I want to be

Some people just don't understand
They just think that friendship should be banned
It is joyful, cheerful and so playful
It makes the world so beautiful

I feel so sad when people are alone
They just sit wanting to cry and moan
I want to go over and say 'Hello'
So they will stop feeling low.

Cara Dee Starr (12)

HOLIDAYS

As I stroll out of the arcade,
A teddy bear I have won,
My eyes gaze upon the view,
Of the sand glistening from the sun.

A child paddling in the ocean,
Candyfloss in her hand,
Her mother watching over her carefully,
Her ears open to the brass band.

I watch the waves crashing down on the shells,
The froth running towards the jagged rock,
The seagulls flying round and round,
As the ships come into the docks.

When the lifeguards get down from their stands,
And the surfers quietly stroll by,
The waves don't crash, just lay still,
And the orange sun sets in the sky.

Liz Gregor (12)

AT BONFIRE NIGHT

At bonfire night
it's a wonderful sight
with the Catherine wheels
that give out squeals.

Rockets take-off
with the clash of bangs
people are all in a group of gangs.

Fireworks take-off from the ground
and they go up and make a terrific sound
I like bonfire night
but sometimes it gives the little ones a
fright!

Gavin Williams (13)

STARS

Those little shimmering, silvery stars
shining in the sky at night.
Those little shimmering, silvery stars
surrounded by moonlight.

I wonder what those shimmering stars
are made of, the ones above my head.
The ones that shine before my eyes
before I go to bed.

I wonder why they only come out at night,
maybe to make the sky look pretty and bright,
or maybe something else.

Those little shimmering, silvery stars
twinkling in the sky.
Those little shimmering silvery stars
make me wonder why.

Danielle Perrett (12)

Evil

As I lie, restlessly, in my bed
I think of the words that evil once said
'When the darkest of night comes, I'll come and get you'
I lie in terror to see if the words are true.

I close my eyes, twitch my fingers
I hear my voice cry out inside of me
As I dart across the room to flick the switch
An ice-cold hand appears, with nails like a witch

The door creaks, light slithers in
A tall dark figure stands before me
I am now halfway between life and death
As I await to breathe my final breath.

Emily King (12)

RUGBY'S PRAYER

Our father who art in Cardiff
Rugby be thy name
Lagers up, punches thrown
Black eyes and broken arms

Give us day by day our breakfast
Before men awake sober
Forgive their sin and lead them
Not to fighting but to friendship

Keelan Bailey (12)

THE MONSTER

I saw the brown monstrous animal
Caged like a prisoner of the law
But when the lights go dim
The poor thing must get out
When the owner comes with more food and fresh water
Mischievous animal comes to a halt
For the hamster will try again
When night returns.

Steven Morgan (12)

THE TWISTERS

The twister is a big thing,
Stronger than a giant.
The twister will pick you up,
And throw you from a height.
Watch out for that twister,
It might give you a fright.

That twister has force,
That is pulling you away.
There are things hitting you,
Getting in your way.
Watch out for that twister,
It will make you scream.

Peter Holmes (12)

I'm Turning!

I'm turning into Dracula,
My teeth are getting thinner,
They're really quite spectacular,
It's hard to eat my dinner.
I'm going off my food a bit
(Except for strawberry jam!)
My mother says I'm batty,
And she's right, I think I am.

Stacey Horton (11)

HALLOWE'EN

She waits one night until quite late,
Steps into the street,
Looks back at the house.
She's hunted down by the spooks and ghouls,
It's a dangerous game of cat and mouse.

Down the street, door to door,
Collecting candy by the score.
She hates this night, it gives her the creeps,
It's not just a game, she's playing for keeps.

Lots of costumes, including her own,
A superhero, a villain, a devil, a queen,
This one night of the year,
It's called Hallowe'en.

Kate Stocking (13)

ALONE

When you're all alone
And there is no one there
You feel scared
But you try not to care

The bumps and the noises
Give you a fright
You're used to these sounds
But not tonight

You close your eyes
And try to dream
But your door abruptly opens
You loudly scream

But no one hears you . . .
But no one hears you . . .

Bethen Richards (13)

CHRISTMAS!

In the snow children go sledging
up and down the slippery road.
It's Christmas, people meeting,
people greeting, people you don't know.
Presents are great, giving and receiving
from friends and family.
Snow on the rooftops, snow on the ground,
wherever you look around.
Friends go meeting in the snow
to go sledging where no one else knows.
Christmas is almost over, make the most of it,
have a great time, and think Christmas
will come another time.
Back in school, you wish you were home
playing in the snow, but think how much
fun you had, but knew it would not last.

Hannah Peacock (12)

CHRISTMAS

Stockings hanging by the fire,
Snowflakes falling every hour.

The lights shining brightly on the Christmas tree,
Sleigh bells ringing just for me.

The stars sparkling in the silvery sky,
Children thinking of Santa with a twinkle in their eye.

When Christmas is over everyone is sad,
But the Happy New Year soon makes them glad.

Eleanor Burchell (13)

LIKES AND DISLIKES

I like toads but I hate roads.
I like chips but I hate ships.
I love my dad except he's mad.
I love my mum except she's dumb.
I hate my brother he's another.
I hate my sister she's a *sister!*

Natalie Hart (12)

BONFIRE NIGHT

Scared I was, until one night,
I sat up and saw the bright lights.
They went up and up in the air,
Blue, red and yellow were the best ones there.
Flashing lights in the sky,
I could hear them everywhere.

Catherine wheels spinning round,
Sparklers sparkling on the ground.
Bang! Terrified I was,
And always will be.

Zoe Cornish (12)

SHIPS

Ships that pass in the night,
Ships that glow in the light.
They make a silent whisper
but can still give you a fright.
Your heart beats faster
when you see the glowing ship.
It docks in the harbour with a gush of
salt water that makes the ship dip.
Ships that pass in the night,
Ships that glow in the light.

Samantha Beynon (13)

MY MOTHER'S CAR

My mother's car is green in colour,
When I get rich I'll buy her another.
My mother's car is a nice little car,
But a Rolls Royce is better by far.

Jason Webber (12)